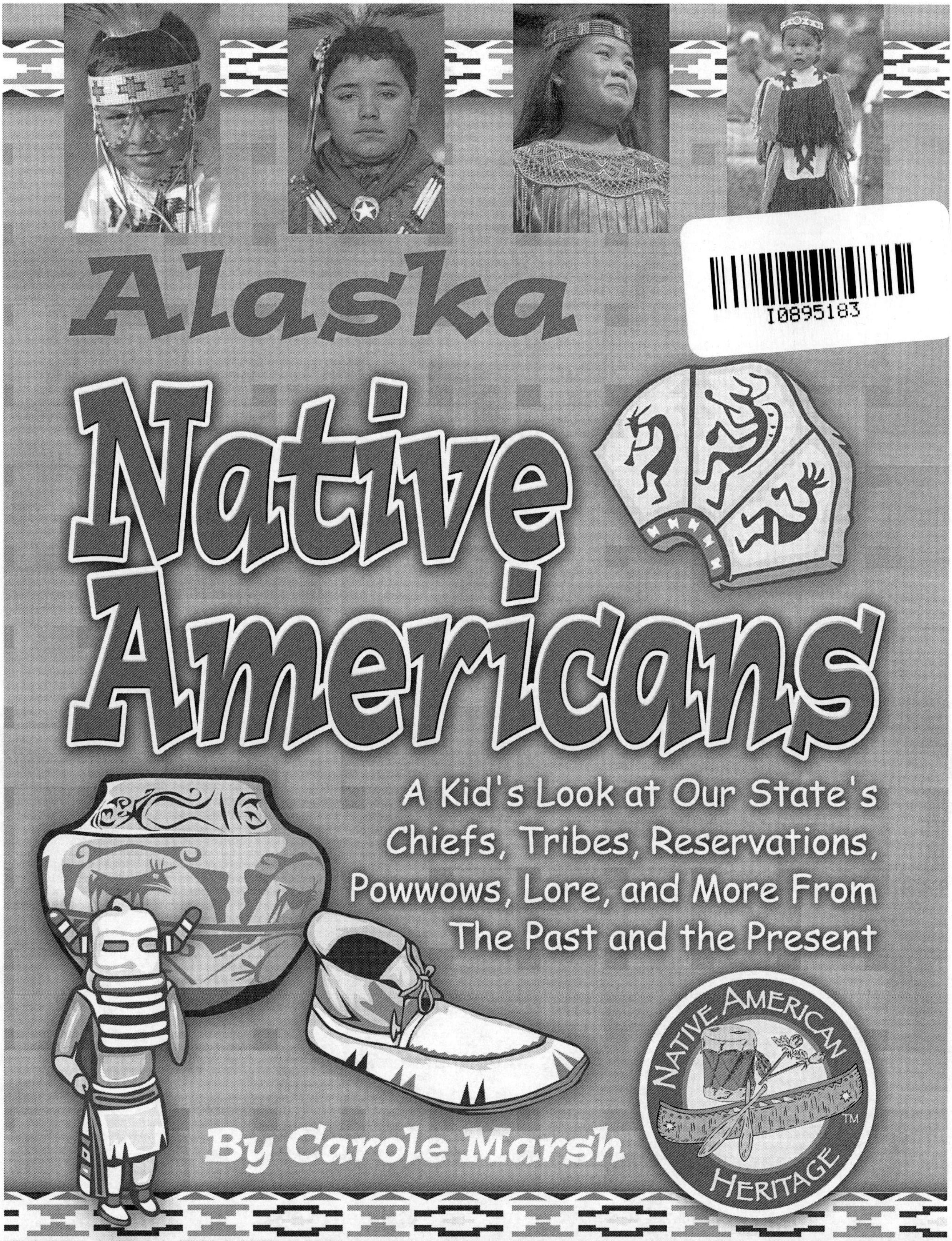

Graphic Design: Lynette Rowe • Cover Design: Victoria DeJoy

Published by
GALLOPADE™ INTERNATIONAL
800-536-2GET
www.gallopade.com

Gallopade is proud to be a member of these educational organizations and associations:

The National School Supply and Equipment Association (NSSEA)
American Booksellers Association (ABA)
Virginia Educational Media Association (VEMA)
Association of Partners for Public Lands (APPL)
Museum Store Association (MSA)
National Association for Gifted Children (NAGC)
Publishers Marketing Association (PMA)
International Reading Association (IRA)
Association of African American Museums (AAAM)

Native American Heritage™ Series

Native American
Big Activity Book

Native American
Biographies

Native American
Coloring Book

Native American
Heritage Book

Native American
Timeline

Alaska State Stuff™

My First Pocket Guide: Alaska
My First Book About Alaska
Alaska Coloring Book
The Big Alaska Reproducible Activity Book
Jeopardy: Answers & Questions About Our State
Alaska "Jography!": A Fun Run Through Our State
Alaska Gamebooks

Alaska Bingo Games
Alaska Illustrated Timelines
Alaska Project Books
Alaska Bulletin Board Set
Alaska PosterMap
Alaska Stickers
Let's Discover Alaska! CD-ROM

Word from the Author

Hello!

I hope you are as interested in North America's wonderful Indian heritage as I am!

Like most kids, I grew up thinking of Indians as the other half of Cowboys. Today, of course, we are getting a much clearer and more accurate picture of what the first peoples on our land were all about. These "facts" are much more fascinating than anything Hollywood can make up. And you probably won't find much of this information in your history textbook!

I am 1/16 Cherokee. This is something I am very proud of and happy about. My grandmother was 1/4 Cherokee. She had tan skin, long gray hair and a very Indian look – especially if I did something bad! Her maiden name was Carrie Corn. Of course, when she got married, she took her husband's name, so it was many years before I learned to appreciate the significance of my native heritage.

Today, I'm trying to make up for lost time by exploring my roots as deeply as I can. One of the most interesting things I've learned is how fascinating all of the Indian tribes are – in the past, the present and future!

As you read about "your" Indians, remember that all native peoples were part of an ever-changing network of time, ideas, power and luck — good and bad. This is certainly a history that is not "dead," but continues to change – often right outside our own back doors! – all the time.

Carole Marsh
She-Who-Writes

PS: Many references show different spellings for the same word. I have tried to select the most common spelling for the time period described. I would not want to be in an Indian spelling bee!

A is for . . .

Alaska

State named for the Aleut word al-ay-es-ka, which means "great land."

Anchorage Museum of History and Art

An entire floor is devoted to Alaska history and native peoples. The Alaska Gallery features complete interior and exterior house scenes for all native peoples.

Aleut and Alutiiq

One of the smallest groups of Alaskan Natives. Live on the Aleutian Islands, the Alaska Peninsula, and the Kenai Peninsula. There are also Aleut settlements on Kodiak Island, the Pribilof Islands of Saint Paul and Saint George, and the Prince William Sound area.

Alaska Native Claims Settlement of 1971

Awarded 44 million acres of land and $962.5 million to Alaska's Inuit, Aleuts and Indians through regional Native corporations. 13 regional native business corporations and more than 200 village corporations were formed. Today, native corporations operate seafood canneries, lumber and pulp mills and mines.

Athabascans

Found in Alaska's great interior. Skilled hunters; tracked moose and caribou through the central forests and plains. Created snowshoes to wear while hunting. Fished for salmon and traded furs and other goods with other native groups. Very nomadic. Traveled by sleds, canoes, and snowshoes.

Alaska Indian Arts Center

Haines; a major native arts and crafts center in the state. Visitors can see native artisans at work on totem poles, tribal masks and silver carving. Totem village, a replica Tlingit village, is nearby.

Arrow

A long, slender shaft made of reed, cane, or wood; pointed tip was attached to one end and split feathers to the other. Feathers helped the arrows fly straight.

Arrowhead

The pointed tip of an arrow, made of bone, antler, wood, or iron. Some tips had barbs that would embed themselves in flesh. These barbs made it difficult for an enemy to remove the arrowhead from a wound.

Alaska State Museum

Juneau; features artifacts from all of the state's primary native cultures. See house posts and carvings, an Eskimo skin boat, rare Chilkat blankets made of mountain-goat wool and cedar bark, and spruce root baskets.

Alaska Native

Although there are 11 different cultural groups, they fall into one of three main groups: Inuit, Aleut, or Indian.

B is for . . .

Beringia

Around 18,000 years ago, during the Ice Age, great masses of land now covered with water were frozen over. This included Beringia or the Bering Land Bridge. This low-lying plain lies beneath the Bering and Chukchi seas today. But once this bridge connected northeastern Siberia in Russia and Alaska. Prehistoric animals and peoples traveled over this bridge.

Blanket Toss

This popular festival spectacle began when Eskimos tossed hunters into the air on walrus skins to spot faraway game. Some were tossed as high as 20 feet into the air!

Baidarkas

Skin-covered kayaks made by the Aleuts.

Barabaras

Winter sod houses supported by whalebone or driftwood; still built by the Aleut Indians.

Bering Land Bridge National Monument

Seward Peninsula; when the waters here froze over to create a land bridge, 13,000 or more years ago, it allowed peoples from the Asian continent to travel into the land that would one day be called Alaska. These people are thought to be the ancestors of all native peoples in the Americas.

Blankets

Used for door covers, partitions, bags, to dry food on, carry babies and many other purposes. Alaska Indians wove blankets from animal hair, skins, bark or feathers.

Barrow

Site of a large Inuit community, 340 miles above the Arctic Circle (northernmost settlement in the U.S.) Here the natives use handmade boats and drying racks in their whaling activities.

Bone

Animal bones were used by Alaska Indians to make buttons, whistles, tools, and also were construction material!

Beads

Made of wood, shells, claws, minerals, seeds — you name it! The Inuit used walrus ivory and animal teeth to make beads.

C is for . . .

Chief

Leader of a tribe. Different titles meant different things. Some members were made chief because they owned deeds to land. Chieftainship was often inherited, usually from the mother!

Canoe

The Indians invented this useful boat, often copied by the white man. Some Haida canoes were 60 feet long, and highly prized by other tribes. Alaskan natives that use the canoe include the Eyak, Tlingit, Haida, Tsimshian, and the Athabascans.

Chilkat Dancers

The Chilkat Dancers perform traditional Northwest Coast dances in full costume in Haines, at the Alaska Indian Arts Center.

Chilkat Blanket

This "blanket" was woven from cedar bark fibers and wool from mountain sheep or goats. Women wove these using their fingers in intricate black, blue-green, yellow and white abstract designs. Shaped like a short chevron with long fringe on the bottom sides. Made by the Tlingit and Tsimshian, and highly prized.

Castle Hill

A National Historic Site, originally a Tlingit settlement in Sitka. Where the American flag was first raised over Alaska in 1867.

Cordova Museum

Prince William Sound; see Chugach and Eyak artifacts.

Clan

A tribal unit. Members are descended from the same ancestor. The most important unit in most Alaska Native groups

Citizenship

The Indian Citizenship Act of 1924 states all Indians born in the United States are citizens of the United States, and citizens of the states they live in, even though they may live on a reservation. They can vote. They pay most local, state and federal taxes, including sales taxes.

Chief Shakes

His tribal house on an island in the harbor at Wrangell is surrounded by a collection of Tlingit totem poles. In the 1800s, he was the leader of the local Stikine clan. His name was handed down from a Tsimshian warrior as part of the spoils of war. His grave here is marked by two carvings of killer whales.

Carrie McLain Memorial Museum

Nome; displays Eskimo artifacts and exhibits about the Bering Strait.

D is for . . .

Dance

Native Alaskan dances can be seen performed by various troupes around the state. The Chilkat Dancers in Haines and the Cape Fox Dancers in Saxman are examples. Eskimos present traditional dances at the Living Museum of the Arctic in Kotzebue. Fairbank's annual Festival of Native Arts also features native dancers.

Descendants

The first Alaska Indians were descendants of primitive hunters who crossed the Bering Strait from Asia to what is now Alaska. At that time, glacial ice still covered most of North America. These people were the true discoverers of the "New World!"

Disease

Alaska Indians had no immunity to the diseases that white explorers, colonists and settlers brought to their lands. These diseases included smallpox, measles, tuberculosis and others, which ravaged the tribes in great epidemics that killed many, and sometimes all, members of a tribe.

Dogs

The Inuit and Athabascans may have been the first Indians to use dogs for transport purposes. Dog teams were used in their daily lives for survival—to haul food back to the villages. Sled dogs of the time were large and could pull heavy weight.

Dyes

Made of lichens, berries, roots, bark, plants, and other natural materials by Indians in Alaska. Different colors were used depending on what materials were available and what objects were to be dyed.

Dillingham Heritage Museum

Alaskan Indian museum featuring southwest Yup'ik Eskimo arts and crafts and Siberian Yup'ik and Inupiaq Eskimo artifacts.

Denali

Athabascan name; means "the high one." Name of the highest peak in North America, located in Alaska's Denali National Park.

Dreams

Important in the Indian tradition. It was believed that dreams were the "windows" to the soul. Many thought a person's hidden desires were expressed in dreams.

E is for . . .

Eagle

Used in many Alaska Indian ceremonies. Feathers were put on war bonnets, rattles, shields, pipes, baskets and prayer sticks. You could tell an Indian's rank in the tribe and the deeds he had done by the kind of feathers he wore and how he wore them.

Ena

A house where women and girls and babies of the Yup'ik and Cup'ik lived. Men and boys lived in a separate house.

Eskimo

The old word used for the Inuit, Inupiaq and the Yupik. Expert hunters and fishers. Live on the islands and coastlands along the Arctic Ocean and Bering Sea. Some live in the Yukon and Kuskokwim river valleys, on Kodiak Island, the southern coast of the Kenai Peninsula and the Alaska Peninsula.

Eklutna

Brightly painted Dena'ina spirit houses mark the graves of an Athabascan burial ground.

Earrings

Medicine men sometimes pierced male and female ears at special ceremonies. Earrings, which cost parents or relatives a significant amount, symbolized wealth and distinction. The more earrings that an Indian wore, the greater his honor. Some earrings measured 12 inches in length!

Environment

Preserving the environment is important to preserving Native American heritage. For thousands of years, Native American tribes lived completely off the land. Farming, mining, pollution have all had a part in changing native environments.

"Eaters of Raw Flesh"

What the word Eskimo is thought to translate to in eastern Canadian Indian language. Most people called Eskimo in the past prefer to be called Inuit today, and historically only ate some of their meat raw.

Epidemics

Few Indians possessed immunity to the deadly diseases, like smallpox and measles, which European explorers and settlers brought to the New World. As a result, great population loss took place. Sometimes entire tribes became extinct. Epidemics sparked by Hernando De Soto's expedition are estimated to have killed 75% of the native population in the New World.

F is for . . .

Fetish

These small objects were thought to hold the spirit of an animal or a part of nature. A fetish could be an object found in nature, such as bone or wood, or it could be a carved object. The fetish was usually small enough to be carried in a small bag or on a cord. The making and use of a fetish was kept secret by its owner and only shared with the one who inherited it.

Food

In the summer, many Alaska Natives ate caribou, musk, oxen and birds. In the winter, they lived on sea mammals, especially seal, whale and fish.

Fort Kenay Historical Museum

On the Kenai Peninsula; features Athabascan and Aleut artifacts.

Food

In the summer, many Alaska Natives ate caribou, musk, oxen and birds. In the winter, they lived on sea mammals, especially seal, whale and fish.

Federal Recognition

The United States government's official acknowledgement of a group of Indians as a tribe that is eligible for government benefits, programs and funds.

Fire-Making

Although fire was necessary to the Indian, some Native Alaskans ate some food raw. Fire was used for cooking and warmth, to harden weapons, thicken rawhide, fell trees, hollow out logs for dugouts, make buckskin and for ceremonies.

Fort Yukon

Located on the Yukon River inside the Arctic Circle. Largest Athabascan village in Alaska. Athabascan women here tan hides, make moccasins and fashion beadwork. A rustic Episcopal church features beadwork altar cloths and hymn books in the Athabascan language.

Fur Trade

In the late 1700s, Russians established a major fur trading operation in Alaska. Native Tlingits resented this invasion by the Russians. In 1802, the Tlingits attacked the Russian settlement, killing most of the Russians and their Aleut slaves. Two years later, the Russians retaliated. For 6 days, the Tlingit bravely fought the Russian troops. But they eventually ran out of ammunition and had to abandon their fortifications in the middle of the night. In the early 1800s, many native Alaskans worked for the Russians on shipbuilding and other construction projects. Others were sent on expeditions up the Yukon and Kuskokwim rivers to find new sources of furs and establish posts.

G is for . . .

Games

Adults played ball and other games of chance or skill. Indian children spun tops, fought pretend battles, did target-shooting, walked on stilts, played hide and seek, or competed to see who could hold their breath the longest!

Gold

In 1880, Tlingit guides unknowingly led prospectors to rich gold deposits along the Gastineau Channel, helping start the gold boom in Alaska.

Gutheni

Tlingit town north of Dry Bay; name means "salmon creek."

Gathering

Native Americans gathered natural materials for food, fuel, baskets, clothing, and housing. American Indian tribes also hunted to meet basic needs. Even though some tribes planted crops, most did some kind of gathering.

Gorgets

Beautiful ornaments hung around the neck or from ears; their significance, if any, is unknown.

Gens

Group of related members from different tribes.

Gates of the Arctic National Park and Preserve

Athabascan Indians live in the park's taiga forestland. Inupiat hunt native caribou herds in the valleys.

Gash

Home of a clan of the Tlingit called Sanyakoan; many of them moved to Ketchikan, Alaska.

H is for . . .

Horn and Hooves

Indians used animal horn to make spoons and dishes. Hooves were made into rattles and bird beaks were used for decoration.

Hankutchin

Known as the "river people." Kutchin group that lived on the Yukon River and were skilled salmon fishermen.

Hair

Indians used hair as a textile. Hair from caribou, mountain sheep, elk, moose, deer, dog, rabbit, beaver, or even humans were used to weave cloth, make wigs, or stuff pillows, balls, dolls or drumsticks.

Haida

These Alaska native Indians live in the towns of Hydaburg and Kasaan in the Prince of Wales Archipelago. Moved into Tlingit territory from Canada in the early 1700s. Recorded information on totem poles. Artists with bones and shells, expert woodworkers, hollowed dugout canoes and built well-constructed clan houses; made bentwood boxes, dugout bowls and spruce-root baskets.

Hunters

Early Indian peoples were hunters who used wooden spears with stone points to kill many kinds of large mammals that are extinct today, such as mammoths and mastodons!

Haines

Located up the Lynn Canal from Juneau. Founded in 1881 as a Presbyterian mission to the native Tlingit people. Haines is the location of the Alaska Indian Arts Center. The Sheldon Museum and Cultural Center has exhibits on Tlingit culture.

Hehlkoan

Tlingit group near Wrangell that belonged to the wolf clan. Name means "people of the foam."

Harpoon

The most important hunting tool for the coastal Alaska Natives. Sometimes used together with sealskin floats to tire out the harpooned animal. Used to hunt seal, walrus, whales, and other marine mammals.

Hootch, Molly

A student from Emmonak. Until 1976, she and other students had to travel to high schools in neighboring villages. A lawsuit filed on her behalf resulted in the Molly Hootch Decree, which says that a high school has to be provided in any community with at least 1 high school-age student.

I is for . . .

Inupiaq

Inuit Natives who live in the north and northwest part of Alaska. From the Arctic Ocean they spread inland to the Brooks Range. The Anaktuvuk Pass is an important Inupiat village.

Ivory-carving

Each summer, Inuit gather in Nome and Kotzebue to market the exquisite carvings they are known for.

Institute of Alaska Native Arts

Fairbanks; provides opportunities for Alaska's Native visual, literary and performing artists through exhibits, workshops, scholarships and internships. Also publishes the Journal of Alaska Native Arts. Founded in 1976.

Inuit

The proper name for the people referred to with the old-fashioned term Eskimo. Includes the Inupiaq and Yupik groups. They can be divided into five main groups: the St. Lawrence Island Yupik, the Bering Strait Inupiat, the Kotzebue Sound Inupiat, the North Alaska Coat Inupiat (Tareumiut), and the North Interior Inupiat (Nunamiut). Contrary to popular belief, most Inuit do not live in igloos. The only Inuit who used igloos are those in north-central Canada.

Indian Reservation

A tract of land set aside by a government for Indians to live on. Alaska's Indians were never forced to live on reservations. After the Alaska Native Claims Settlement Act of 1971, only one remains in the entire state.

Iqyax

The native name for an Aleut kayak. They are different from other kayaks because they have a split bow for speed and stability.

Indian Tribes/Native Groups in Alaska

At one time or another, these native people have lived in the state of Alaska: Aleut, Athabascans, Alutiiq, Cup'ik, Eyak, Haida, Inupiaq, Inuit, Kutchin, St. Lawrence Island Yupik. Tlingit, Tsimshian, Yup'ik.

Indian

In 1493, Christopher Columbus called the native people he met in North America "Indians" because he mistakenly believed he had sailed to India! Today, this term includes the aborigines of North and South America.

J is for . . .

Just So You Know . . .

Today you can find many Alaska Indians that follow some traditional ways. But there are also many who are entrepreneurs, doctors, lawyers, educators and even politicians! If you visit a reservation or cultural event, make sure you know visitor etiquette. Often dances are religious ceremonies and should be observed as such; religious dances should not be applauded. Photography, videotaping and drawing are all important issues - check with the tribe or individual before any is started.

Jobs

Alaska's Natives work at all types of jobs. Some are commercial seal hunters or fishermen. Many maritime Indians work in the fishing, logging, lumbering and pulp industries. Still others work in cities at careers as diverse as accounting to zoology. Some work from computers at home, communicating around the world.

Justice?

For hundreds of years, Native Americans have not received justice from federal and state governments. Native Americans have had nearly all their land taken away. Native Americans still have to fight for their rights in courts across the land.

Judicial Termination

Modern term to describe current efforts by various U.S. government agencies and officials (especially the judicial system) to legally decrease the sovereignty of independent Indian tribes.

Just In Time!

The Indian Arts and Crafts Act of 1990 makes it against the law to pretend that an item has been made by Native Americans if it is really not. It is illegal to offer or display for sale, or sell any art or craft product in a way that falsely suggests it is Indian produced.

Juneau

At the head of Seward Street in Alaska's capital, stands a totem, which according to local tradition, brings good luck if you touch it.

K is for . . .

Ketchikan

Site of the largest collection of totem poles in the world. See them in Saxman Indian Village, Totem Bight State Historical Park and the Totem Heritage Center.

Kutchin

These Indians had ancestral territory in Alaska, from the Yukon east into Canada. They hunted, fished, used Inuit-style sleds and also birch-bark canoes. Some Kutchin can be found in Athabascan villages today.

Kotzebue

Inupiat Inuit make up more than 75% of this community's population. Lies within the Arctic Circle. Many residents here still use fish-drying racks and handmade fishing boats. At the Living Museum of the Arctic, you can hear the famous Kotzebue Eskimo singers. The Jade Mountain Products plant features jade jewelry crafted by native artisans. Site of a spring beluga (white) whale hunt using umiaks and kayaks. Whale meat is later hung on racks in the streets to dry.

Knife

Made from various materials such as bone, reed, stone, wood, antler, shell, metal, or animal teeth (bear, beaver, etc.), knives were used as weapons but also creative handiwork.

Koniag Indians

A large number of them were killed, and others taken hostage, when Grigori Shelikof established a Russian post near Three Saints Bay on Kodiak Island in 1784.

Knots

Tied on bowstrings, spearhead and arrowhead lashings, snowshoes, and other items, knots were sometimes used to keep track of the days like a calendar—each knot equaled 1 day.

L is for . . .

Lamps

Alaska Natives used a variety of lamps for heating, cooking, and light. Most used fish or sea mammal oil for fuel.

Leggings

Both men and women wore cloth or skin covering, which were often decorated with quills, beads, or painted designs, for their legs.

Lost Tribes of Israel

This historic theory has been floating around since 721 BC. The 10 lost tribes of Israel are supposedly groups of people gathered together by Sargon, the King of Assyria. Some say he cast out 10 of the 12 tribes of Israel. Many have tried to prove that the American Indians are these missing tribes!

Leister

A special fishing harpoon with three prongs used by Arctic natives. One prong speared the fish while the other two held it.

Lodge

The term for a type of Indian house that was usually a permanent dwelling. The population of a tribe was often estimated by its number of lodges.

Lifestyle

Some of Alaska's native peoples still carry on a subsistence lifestyle. For many Inuit and Aleut, survival depends on hunting and processing whales, walruses and seals. They use the meat, hides and fat for food, clothing, heating, fuel, tools and home-building materials. Other native peoples have moved to cities and adapted to non-native lifestyles and jobs. Many combine old and new ways in their lives, such as fishing from native boats while using whaling guns and walkie-talkies.

Land Loss

Native Americans lost their land in many ways. Conflicts with other tribes, colonization, European settlement, treaties, and removal took away Indian lands.

Lance

Spear used for hunting and war. The hunting lance had a short shaft and a broad, heavy head. The war lance was light and had a long shaft.

Labret

An Inuit lip or chin plug, worn as jewelry. Made from shell, ivory, wood, or stone.

M is for . . .

Masks

A face covering made from wood, basketwork, pottery or hides. Alaska Indians carved, painted and decorated masks with shells, fiber, hair, or feathers. Each mask had a special meaning. Wood masks are especially common in Alaska.

Mukluks

Inuit snow-boots, often made of sealskin, insulated with moss and down.

Missions

Many religious groups who came to Alaska to try to assist the native peoples. They wanted to convert them to their religion, as well as help them adapt to the white man's ways.

Medicine

Medicine could be good or bad. Medicines or charms were placed in a bag by young warriors and carried at all times. Some of the roots, leaves and bark that Indians in our state used as medicine are being rediscovered and used by today's doctors!

Moccasins

Indian shoes made of animal skin. The boot or legging-moccasin is common in Alaska.

Medicine Man

A person who got the power to heal the sick through a secret means, usually from a dream or visions.

Moved Out

In World War II, the Japanese attacked the Aleutian Islands and removed many natives to Japan. The U.S. evacuated the remaining Aleut, moving them to abandoned canneries on the mainland. Many died from lack of fuel, starvation, and disease. Find out more at the Aleutian World War II national Historic Area on Amaknak Island.

N is for . . .

Nomads

Bands of these roving people migrated across the Bering Strait and the Bering Sea. They crossed Alaska in search of fish, game and edible plants. Early Eskimos stalked caribou and musk-oxen in the northern tundra. They hunted walruses, seals, polar bears and birds. From skin-covered boats called kayaks, they harpooned whales to use the fat or blubber for cooking and heating fuel.

Notable Crafters

Alaska's Tsimshian were accomplished in the arts and crafts. They were known for their button blankets. After getting European buttons, they began making animal clan shapes by attaching hundreds of mother-of-pearl buttons!

Nation

There are many Indian nations located within the United States, such as the Haida Nation. Indian nations are called nations because their governments and laws are independent of and separate from the U.S. government. The federal government must have "government to government" relations with these Indian nations, just as it would with foreign nations, like England or Spain.

November

In 1990, President George Bush approved a joint resolution designating November 1990 "National American Indian Heritage Month." Similar proclamations have been issued each year since 1994.

Names

Indian names were often changed during one's lifetime. These names could be derived from events that happened during the person's birth, childhood, adolescence, war service, or retirement from active tribal life. Some names came from dreams, some were inherited, and sometimes names were stolen or taken in revenge. Today some Indians maintain old, traditional Indian names, while others take modern names. Since settlers often did not read or write Indian languages, they recorded Indian names phonetically (as they "sounded"). Thus Indian names were often misspelled.

Numbers of Natives

Alaska's native peoples make up about 19% of the state's population today. The largest Native group is the Yup'ik, with a population of over 20,000. There are around 1,400 of the smallest group, the Tsimshian. Around 12,000 Alaska natives are Athabascan. About 9,000 Tlingit and Haida people live in Alaska, 14,500 Inupiat, and 3,900 Aleut.

Nome

About 51% of this Alaska city's residents are Alaska Natives. The city may have gotten its name from the Eskimo phrase kn-no-me, or "I don't know." This was supposed to have been the natives' answer when asked the name of this place. Here you can see native artists carve beautiful sculptures from walrus-tusk ivory.

O is for . . .

Organization

The Alaska Native Brotherhood/Sisterhood was founded in 1912 as an inter-tribal organization. Several Tlingit and a Tsimshian founded it in Sitka.

Over the Snow

Native peoples developed snowshoes for winter travel on top of the snow. Used by the Inuit, Kutchin, and other groups. In fact, the Kutchin snowshoes are unique–they are very narrow and can be up to six feet long!

Origins

Some scientists believe that Native Americans actually came across a land bridge between Asia and North America. They say that during an ice age thousands of years ago, the water level was much lower and people could have walked between the two continents.

One Sky Productions

Anchorage; producers of "Heartbeat Alaska" and "One Sky" television programs. They also teach videography and have a curriculum program!

Oil

Alaska Natives and Indians used oil for heating, cooking, and light. Oil came from fish like the candlefish, land mammals like bears, or sea mammals like seals and whales.

Orators

Many Indian leaders were excellent public speakers. Powerful and dramatic speakers were vital to leaders who wanted to influence their tribe. Watch for famous Indian quotations in literature and textbooks!

Office of Indian Education Programs

This is a service organization devoted to providing quality education opportunities for American Indian people. Established in the latter part of the nineteenth century to carry out the federal government's education commitment to Indian tribes, it has become the only national education system for American Indian children and adults.

P is for . . .

Powwow

The original form of the word meant "medicine man." Medicine men would often use noise motion and confusion to scare away harmful spirits and cure people. It was also a gathering to talk about political matters. Today, the powwow is an event where Indians gather to sing, perform ceremonial dances, and share cultural pride and traditions.

Potlatch

A ceremony or feast where the host gives away many of the things he owns to prove wealth. In the past, sometimes gifts were expected in return from the guests. Practiced by the Haida, Tlingit, and Tsimshian.

Petroglyph Beach State Historic Park

Located in Wrangell; here you can see ancient Indian rock carvings.

Paint

Indians used many natural materials to make paint, like clay mixed with oil or grease. Yellow "paint" was made with the gall bladder of a buffalo! Why did they paint their faces or bodies? Indians used paint to look scary or beautiful, to disguise themselves, or to protect their skin from sunburn or insect bites. Indians often applied red paint because it symbolized strength and success. That is why settlers often referred to the Indians as Red Men.

Parka

This is a traditional Alaska Native winter garment. It comes in many variations. It has a hood and was made out of skins, with the fur facing in. Sometimes they were even decorated!

Pemmican

Indian food made of animal meat, which was dried in the sun, pounded together with fat and berries. The mixture was packed into skin bags and used primarily while on the trail.

Paleo-Indians

Prehistoric peoples who crossed the Bering Land Bridge to hunt woolly mammoths, steppe bisons, miniature horses, mastodons, antelopes, musk-oxen, moose, camels, sloths, lions and saber-toothed tigers with weapons made from chipped stone.

Pratt Museum

Homer; includes displays of Dena'ina, Aleut, and Pacific Eskimo artifacts.

Pottery

Indian pottery was made from built-up spirals of clay that were molded or paddled, or a combination of the two methods. Most pottery served as cooking vessels.

Q is for . . .

Quillwork

Indians used the quills of porcupine or birds to make a type of embroidery. Quills were dyed with juice from berries and other materials. When they were ready to be used, the quills were either mashed with teeth or softened with hot water and flattened with rocks. The quills were then laced into moccasins, shirts, pipe covers, and other items. Beads which Indians received by trading with settlers eventually replaced quillwork.

Quality

Alaska Native arts and crafts are known for their excellent craftsmanship and striking designs. This work is often influenced by things found in nature, especially plants and animals.

Quiver

Case used to hold arrows; made of woven plant materials or animal skins.

Qiipaghaq

This is a traditional Inupiaq/Yupik piece of clothing. It is the outer pullover top that goes over the inner pullover, which is a parka.

Qitiks

Christmas festival in Barrow, North America's northernmost community. Includes mukluk races, Eskimo games, dancing and dog races.

R is for . . .

Red Dog Mine

Owned by the Northwest Arctic Native Association. These zinc deposits in the northern region near Kotzebue are the largest unmined zinc reserves in the world.

Roots

Indians used plant roots for food, medicine, dye, baskets, cloth, rope, salt, flavoring, and just to chew!

Rattles

Indians of Alaska made rattles from bird beaks, animal hooves, bones, pods, seashells, turtle shells and other animal parts. The rattles are used in ceremonies.

Rawhide

Untanned animal hide. The "green" hide was stretched on the ground or over a frame. Flesh and fat were removed. The skin was dried, washed, then buried with wood ashes which made the hair come off. Used by the Alaska Indian to make drumheads, lash lodge poles, mend broken objects and in many other ways.

"Rondy"

Short for rendezvous; a unique Alaska celebration, often of native cultures and history.

Reservations

The U.S. government set aside, or "reserved," land for the Indians. These reservations originally served as a sort of prison during the beginning stages of Indian removal. At that time, reservations provided the government with some control over Indian activity and residency. This land was usually considerably less desirable land than the Indians' native territories. Today's reservations are lands that are tribally held, yet protected by the government.

"Ridicule Pole"

Located in Haines; built to shame a debtor into paying his bills!

S is for . . .

Sheldon Jackson Museum

Sitka; established in 1887. Oldest museum in Alaska. One of the best collections of artifacts for Alaska's native cultures. The missionary the museum is named for collected most of the basketry, clothing, carvings, necklaces and masks.

Sign Language

A way for Indians to communicate with others from a tribe whose language they did not speak.

Shaman

Medicine man and spiritual leader who was supposed to have special healing power from another world.

Slaves

Aleut Indians were used as slaves by Russians in the mid-1700s. Because they were expert hunters, they were forced to work for the Russians and pay taxes in furs. The Russians almost exterminated the Aleut population of 25,000. By the end of the 1700s, only 2,000 Aleuts were left.

Southeast Alaska Indian Cultural Center

Sitka; displays native arts including woodcarving, silverwork, costumes and robes.

Simon Paneak Memorial Museum

Anaktuvuk Pass; features the Nunamiut or inland Eskimos of the Central Brooks Range.

Sacred Bundles

A group of objects treasured by a tribe. They were well-guarded and often taken into battle. The items were publicly shown only on very important occasions.

Seward Peninsula

Site of the Bering Land Bridge National Monument, where the ancestors of all native American peoples probably entered the Americas about 13,000 or more years ago.

Sitka

Alaskan city rich in Tlingit culture. At the Sitka National Historical Park you can visit a cultural center for Indian history and art, and a Tlingit totem park. It marks the spot where the Tlingit made their last stand in 1804. Nothing remains of the fort they built to protect themselves. Tlingit and Haida totem poles mark the trail to the fort site. The visitor center features native ornamental objects, blankets, baskets and working craftspeople.

Samuel K. Fox Museum

Dillingham; southwest Yup'ik Eskimo arts and crafts plus Siberian Yup'ik and Inupiaq Eskimo artifacts.

Saxman

Tlingit village where native performers present their customs, history, myths and songs at the Naa Kahidi Theater.

T is for . . .

Tongass Historical Museum

Ketchikan; Displays of Haida, Tlingit and Tsimshian tools, baskets and ceremonial objects.

Tlingit Tribal House of the Bear

Chief Shakes Island; reproduction of a Tlingit community house, great cedar buildings where 50-100 people lived together in the winter.

Tsimshian

These native Alaska Indians live at Matlakatla on Annette Island. They have ocean villages and are known for their woodworking, weaving and basketry.

Totem

The spirit of some natural object (usually an animal) taken by an Indian, tribe or family to guard over them.

Thule

Sea-mammal hunting culture of the Eskimo around 1,000 years ago.

Totem Poles

One of the most famous Alaskan native art forms. Carved from red cedar and used as house supports, memorials or to indicate status and clan relationships. Stand up to 80 feet high. Today, skilled craftspeople train with master carvers to learn this ancient art.

Tlingit

These native Indians live on the Alaska Panhandle. In this mild climate, they found plentiful fish, game and edible plants. Also enjoyed a very developed cultural and artistic life, creating totem poles, intricate ceremonial garments and exquisite blankets. They are also expert woodworkers.

Teeth

Alaska Indians hung teeth on cords to make necklaces.

Tribe

A group of Indians with shared culture, history, original territory, ancestry, social organization, and governmental structure. A tribe may contain several bands of Indians.

Thunderbird

A mythological Indian figure, as well as a part of the constellations for many Indians. Thunderbird mythology is mostly different from tribe to tribe, in general either coexisting with ancestors as an actual bird, or appearing as a spiritual nature god. The Thunderbird was good to the people in either case. Much mythology ties the thunderbird with thunder, lightning and storms.

Tattoo

At maturity, some Native girls had a line tattooed at the edge of their lower lip. When she married, 2 more lines were added. Native men sometimes kept a tally of the number of whales they had killed by using tattoo marks on their cheeks, chests or arms. Many other Alaska Native men bore clan tattoos on their chests.

U is for . . .

U.S. Bureau of Indian Affairs

Provides public services such as law enforcement, land records, economic development, and education to Indians. Known for mismanagement and ethical problems.

U.S. Army

Many Native Americans have fought bravely for the United States Army. Many have also given their lives for a country that was not always accepting of them.

Unique

Each and every tribe has its own unique customs, language, and traditions.

Umiaks

Large open, wood-frame boats covered with skins. Used by the Inupiaq to hunt whales and walrus, plus travel and trading. Some could be as long as 50 feet!

U.S. Indian Reorganization Act

Passed by Congress in 1934, the act authorized Indian tribes to establish and conduct their own governments, and to form businesses.

Uluaq

A versatile fan-shaped slate knife, an important tool in Yup'ik and Cup'ik households.

University of Alaska Museum

Fairbanks; has fine archaeological, paleontological, geographical and ethnological collections, including Athabascan basketry, Eskimo carving, and Tlingit and Haida potlatch items.

Unalaska

An ancient Aleut village and center of activity during Russian occupation.

V is for . . .

Vessels

Indians carried water in special gourds, skins, or pottery shaped liked bottles, called water vessels.

Village Councils

These were held in the town (council) house and occurred to discuss and decide important matters. Harmony and agreement was essential to tribal unity. Rather than vote on issues, they were discussed until everyone was satisfied. Anyone who wanted to could speak freely. Everyone did not always agree on the outcome, but everyone avoided conflict by pushing their case.

Vegetable Dyes

Indians could not buy color from the store like we can today. Instead, they created many different colors from the things they found on earth like plants, flowers, shrubs, trees, roots, and berries. They made beautiful and unique reds, oranges, yellows, greens, browns, and violets. These dyes were used for baskets, pottery, weaving, body makeup, and clothing.

Very Hungry

There were Indians who here hunters, gatherers and foragers, that often ate whatever they could find! How hungry would you have to be to eat what they sometimes ate: reptiles, larvae, and insects?

Villages

Many Alaska Indians lived in villages! Villages were formed around different clans or bands within the tribe, but could also contain different clans living together. Villages were usually permanent settlements, although semi-nomadic tribes have been known to migrate between permanent villages.

Vesperic Indians

Indian tribes located in the United States.

W is for . . .

World Eskimo Indian Olympics

Held in Fairbanks each summer, along with the Festival of Native Arts. Many of the Native events are historical games that helped develop survival skills in Alaska's harsh climate.

Weirs

Natives built these enclosures in shallow waters from stones or brush that were used to catch fish.

Wasilla Museum

Wasilla; features Indian baskets.

Wickersham Courthouse

Eagle City; the museum here features local Indian relics.

Walrus

Another important sea mammal to Alaska's native peoples. They are summer game. Besides providing food and skins, their ivory tusks are used for arts and crafts, tools, and weapons.

Whales

Not all Inuit hunt whales, but many still hunt whales today. A large whale could feed an entire village for a year, and was also an important source for oil, bone, and sinew used in fuel, tools, construction and clothing. The killer whale is considered sacred by many native people.

Whistle

Indians from Alaska made them from the wing bones of birds. The whistles made the sound of the bird the bones came from! Used to communicate, signal, sound an alarm or even flirt with a maiden!

Wrangell

Site of ancient Indian rock carvings, visible along the beach at low tide.

White Man

Indians generally called them Pale Face, a name the white men themselves suggested!

Woodworkers

Alaska's southeast native peoples are amazing woodworkers. The Haida were the most highly skilled. They made huge dugouts, totem poles, cedar plank houses, cedar chests and even wooden boxes to cook in!

XYZ are for . . .

Xenophobe

A xenophobe is someone who is afraid of foreign people, their customs and cultures, or foreign things. Many of the first European settlers were afraid of Native American cultures.

Yupiit Piciryarait Cultural Center and Museum

Bethel; Yup'ik Eskimo artifacts of southwest Alaska, including baskets clothes, utensils, ceremonial items, masks and more.

Yupik or Yup'ik

Alaska Natives who live in western Alaska, along the Bering Sea. Historically they were very nomadic. Hunted and gathered for food, both on the land and at sea.

ZZZZZZ...

Shamans and medicine men were not the only people who had access to the spirit world. Indians believed that people could make contact with spirits every night in their dreams! Dreamers could travel back to the time of man's creation or far ahead into their own futures. They also believed that dreams contained warnings or commands from the spirits. Many tribes felt that they had to act out their dreams as soon as they awoke. If an Indian dreamed about bathing, for example, he would run to his neighbors' houses first thing in the morning, and his neighbors would throw kettles full of cold water over him.

Y... Or, "Why?"

1. Why do you think Indian warriors carried charms with them? Some Indian medicines have been scientifically proven to have true healing power and are still used today. Do you think their charms had any real power to help them win battles?
2. Why do you think the American government kept relocating Indians onto reservations and then making the reservations smaller and smaller?
3. Why did Indians use items such as a pipe in ceremonies? What kinds of symbolic objects do we use in ceremonies today?
4. Why and how did Indians use natural materials in creative ways?
5. Many Indian tribes are running successful businesses on their reservations today. There is one industry that many tribes are making a lot of money at. Do you know what this is? Hint: "I'll bet you do!"

Which Famous Native American Am I?

Solve the puzzle!

Word Bank

Black Elk	Crazy Horse	Sitting Bull	Sequoia
Sacajawea	Chief Joseph	Geronimo	Pocahontas

Down

1. This Shoshone woman joined Lewis and Clark as their guide and translator and helped make the expedition a success! Hint: She has 4 "a"s in her name!
4. This man gave the Cherokee their first alphabet so that they could write. Until then, they communicated only by speaking and drawing pictures. Hint: A famous ancient tree also has the same name!
5. He was one of the fiercest of Indian warriors! He fought against white settlers in Arizona and New Mexico to keep his people from being pushed off their lands. Hint: Jump!

Across

2. A legend says that this brave Algonquian woman saved the life of Englishman John Smith. Hint: Disney produced a movie about her.
3. He fought at Little Bighorn when he was only 13! He was also a wise "shaman" who saw visions and could advise people. Hint: Part of his name is an animal with antlers!
6. He was a great Sioux warrior who won the battle against General Custer at Little Bighorn in 1876. Hint: His horse was not crazy!
7. A leader of the Lakota (Sioux) tribe who lived on the Standing Rock Reservation in North Dakota after the battle of Little Bighorn. He tried to make conditions better for his people there, so the U.S. government called him a "troublemaker." Hint: He did not sit all the time!
8. A wise and brave chief of the Nez Percé who tried to bring his people to Canada to escape war. He said, "From where the sun now stands, I will fight no more forever." Hint: His father's name was "Old Joseph."

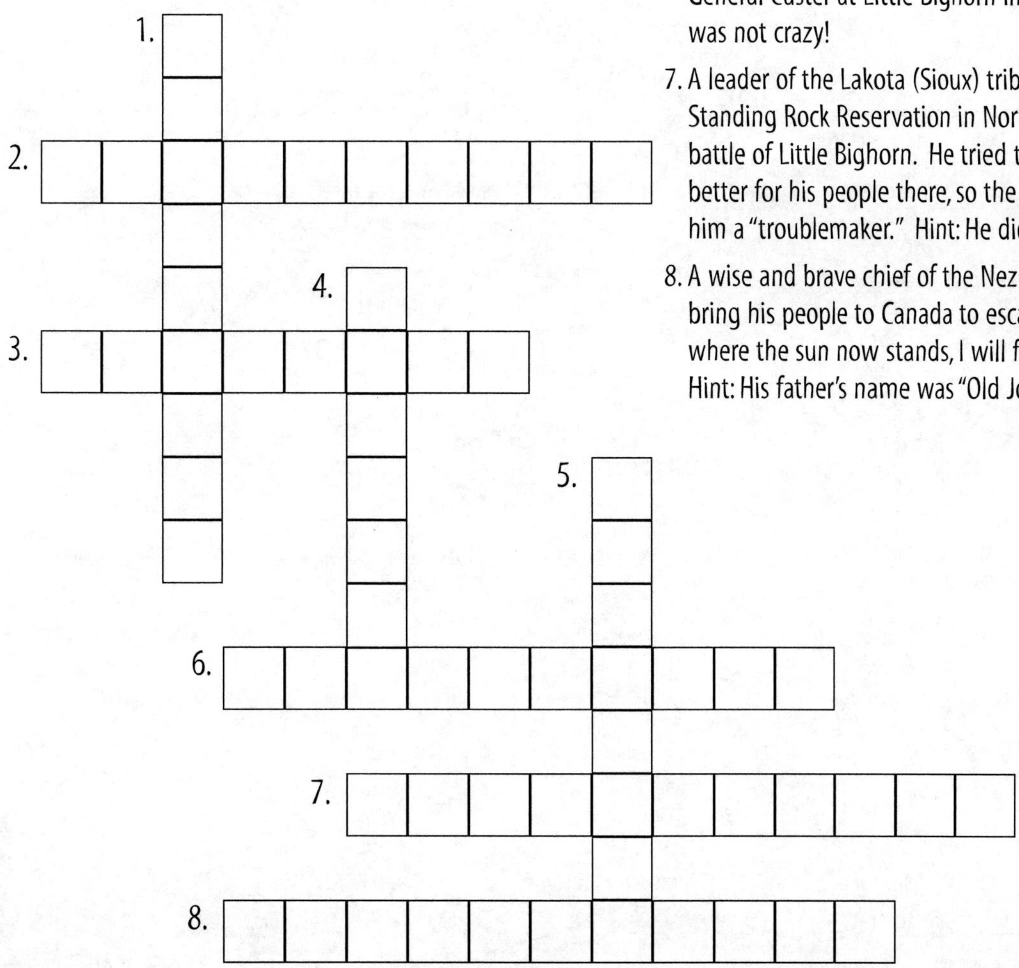

Answer Key: 1. Sacajawea; 2. Pocahontas; 3. Black Elk; 4. Sequoia; 5. Geronimo; 6. Crazy Horse; 7. Sitting Bull; 8. Chief Joseph

Different Ways for Different Indians!

North American Indian tribes are divided into different areas. In each of these areas, tribes shared common ways of living with each other. They might make similar arts or crafts, they might eat the same foods, or they might have had the same beliefs. These activities are all part of their "culture." Each area had its own culture, which was different from the tribes in all the other areas.

Below is a map of all the different groups of Indian tribes in North America. Color each area with a different color. You will see a colorful picture of how Native Americans can all be called "Indians" but still have very different cultures!

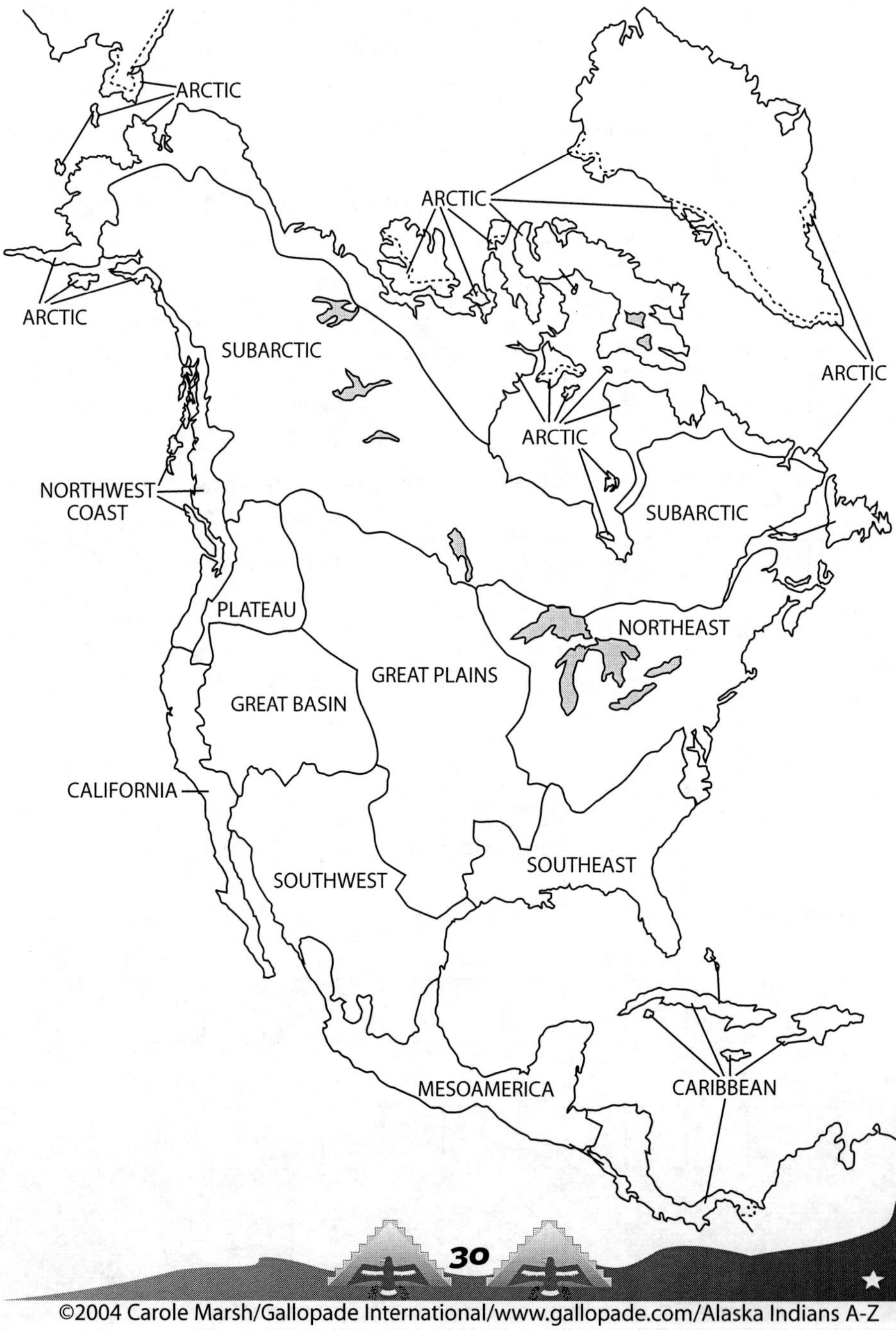

Celebration!

Powwows are big festivals where Native Americans gather to sing, dance, and eat together. It is a time to celebrate and show pride in their culture. Powwows can last from one afternoon to several days. The Indians dress in native costumes and dance ancient dances to the beating of drums.

Artists sell their arts and crafts. You might be able to buy some real Native American food cooked on an open fire. Native Americans go to powwows to be with each other, share ideas, and just have fun! Most powwows are also open to people who are not Indian. It's a great place to learn about Native American culture!

If you went to a powwow this weekend, what do you think you would see? What do you think might NOT be there? Circle the objects you think you would see at a powwow. Put an X through those you probably won't see.

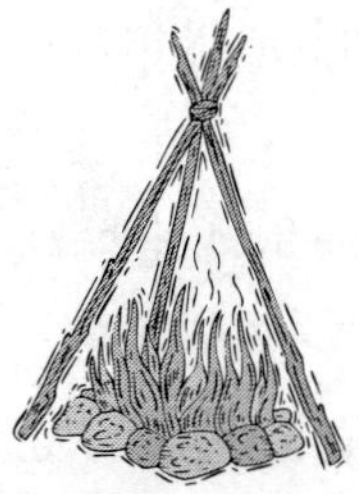

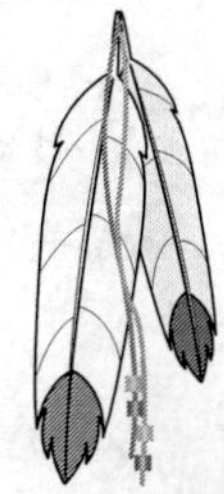

Answer Key: Circled objects are: beads, moccasins, open fire, drums, feathers, baskets, kids, food, drums, horse.

Make an Indian Weaving!

Many Native Americans used weaving to create useful things like sashes (belts), bags, mats, and blankets. They used animal hair to make yarn, and dyed the yarn with natural dyes from fruits and other plants. They also used some plant fibers, like cotton, to make weaving thread.

Weave a small Native American mat of your own. Use different colors of yarn to create a beautiful pattern in your weaving. Place a favorite object on the mat or hang it on your wall!

Prepare the "loom"

Cut a piece of cardboard 5 inches wide and 6 inches long. Along the two 5-inch sides (the "short" sides), have an adult cut slits 1/4 inch deep. These slits should be 1/2 inch apart from each other. So, on each short side you will have 9 slits.

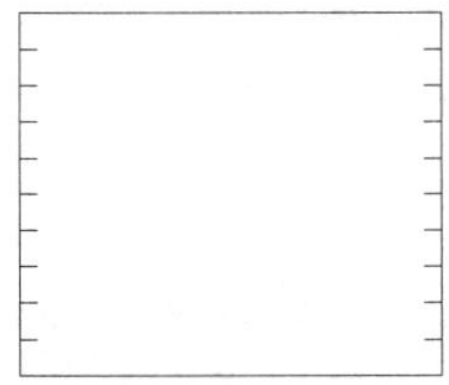

Directions:

1. Take a long piece of yarn and bring it from the back through the first slit (the one next to the edge of the cardboard.) The end of the yarn will hang down behind the cardboard.

2. Bring the yarn right across the front of the cardboard to the slit opposite the one your yarn came through.

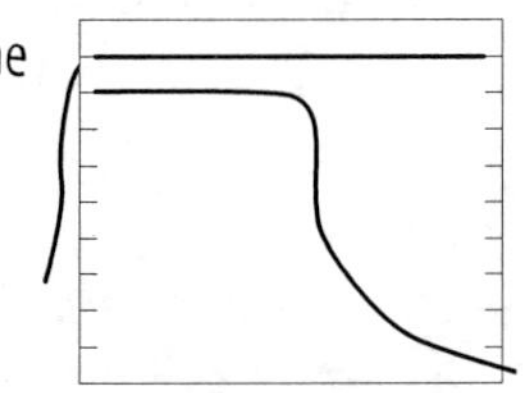

3. Now bring the yarn under the back of the cardboard and then up again through the second slit.

4. Repeat #2 and #3, until you have 9 strands of yarn across the front of your cardboard!

5. Then cut the yarn and tie the two loose ends in the back of the cardboard.

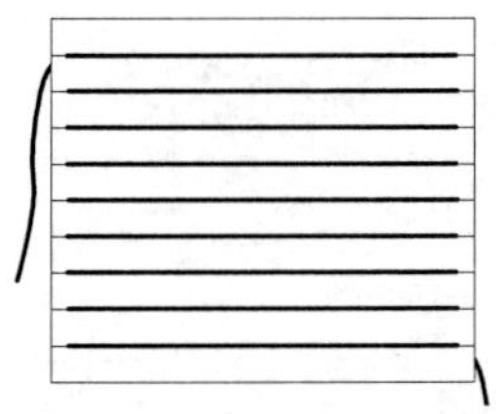

6. Take another piece of yarn and start feeding it through the 9 strands, going over one, under the next over the next, etc. When you get to the end, pull the yarn behind the cardboard and around to the front, and begin again. This time, whatever strand you went over, go under. And whatever strand you went under, go over.

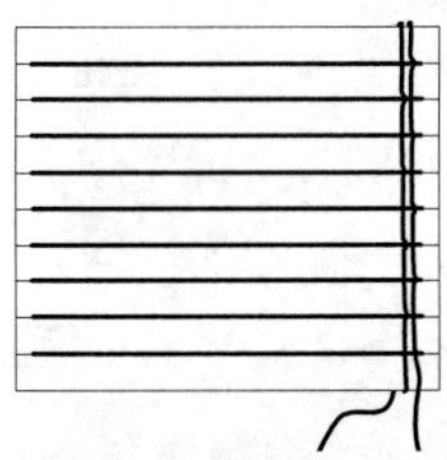

7. Repeat this pattern until the front of your cardboard in covered. Then cut the yarn in the back of the cardboard, and trim it to create a fringe for your mat!

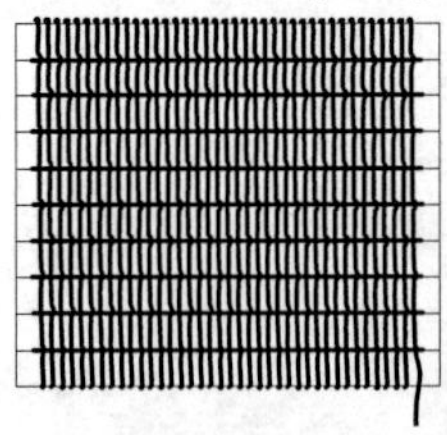

Tips:

- For a wild look, use variegated or different colored yarn!
- For a tighter mat, push the under/over strands up against the previous strands during weaving.
- To keep your mat from unravelling, tie neighboring fringe together up close to the mat.

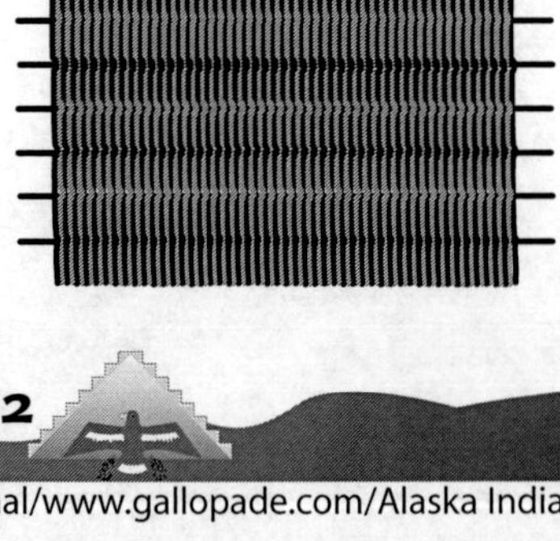

Finders Keepers?

Native Americans have many buried treasures. For hundreds of years, special objects would sometimes be buried with Native Americans, or maybe they would just be lost. Archeologists used to dig for interesting artifacts in old Native American gravesites. They would keep the Native American bones or the arrowheads, rattles, masks and other objects that they found. But this made the Native Americans feel like they were being robbed.

In 1990, the U.S. government passed a law that said that no one could look for or take these Native American objects anymore. And whoever had any already had to give them back to the people they belonged to. This is called repatriation

Help the archeologist return the artifact to a Native American.

Fast Fact

An artifact is an object that was made by people a long time ago for some useful purpose.

Busy Hands!

Before modern times, Native Americans didn't have stores where they went to buy things. They made everything they needed.

What did Indians make with their own hands? Use the Word Bank and pictures to find out!

Word Bank

blanket	moccasins	arrows	pottery	canoe
mat	food	jewelry	pouch	box

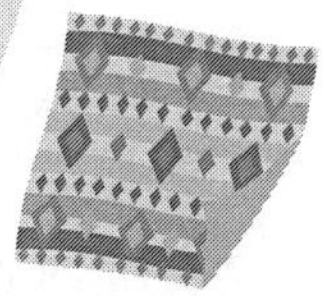 ___ ___ ___

 ___ ___ ___ ___

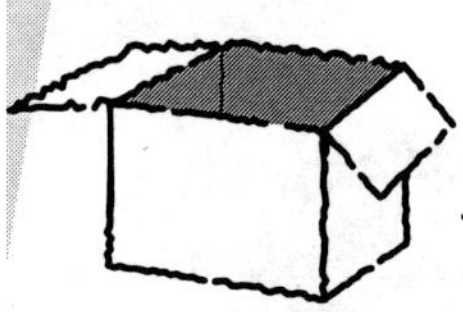 ___ ___ ___

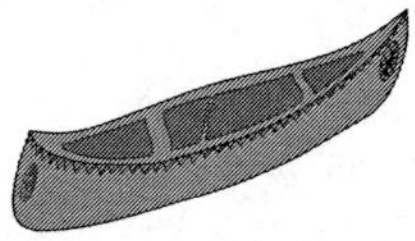 ___ ___ ___ ___ ___

 ___ ___ ___ ___ ___ ___ ___

 ___ ___ ___ ___ ___

 ___ ___ ___ ___ ___ ___ ___ ___ ___ ___

 ___ ___ ___ ___ ___ ___

 ___ ___ ___ ___ ___ ___ ___

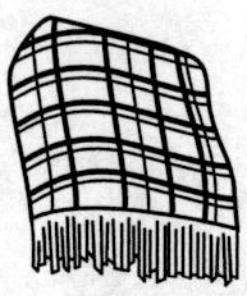 ___ ___ ___ ___ ___ ___ ___

American Indians Today

Beginning with the first letter of each group of letters, cross out every other letter to discover some new words. You may not have heard of these before, but you can read all about them!

1. Many Indians live on these, but many more do not!

TRYELSDEBRNVJAOTPIPOWNASX

____

2. Many Indians have been poor for a long time because for many years the government took away their lands and their ability to make a living.

TPKOOVWEBRNTXYA

____

3. Many Indians have been studying hard at school and going to college in order to earn more money. Education helps the Indians make their lives better. These Native Americans are working to become:

TSJUMCBCFEYSMSOFPUVL

____

4. This is a big term that means Native Americans have worked hard to get the U.S. government to let them rule themselves. This means that they have their own laws and make their own decisions. They are like a separate country inside the U.S.! Now, try and see if you can get your parents to give you the same thing!

TSGENLBF JDGEETSEWRAMCIHNUAKTYIKOTNU

_____________ _______________________________

Fast Fact

What do Indians work as today?

- doctors
- nurses
- factory workers
- artists
- lawyers
- actors

The same kinds of jobs any American might work at!

Native Americans Move to the City!

Solve the code to discover the mystery words!

A	B	C	D	E	F	G	H	I	J	K	L	M
✳	❀	⌘	♣	➸	♥	❗	✯	✂	✆	☛	✈	✉
N	**O**	**P**	**Q**	**R**	**S**	**T**	**U**	**V**	**W**	**X**	**Y**	**Z**
✿	☆	✦	✡	✏	❦	☎	✒	✙	✗	✍	✠	✓

1. During the 1950s and 1960s, the American government paid Indians to leave their homes on reservations and move to cities to get jobs. If cities are sometimes called urban areas, then these brave Indians were called:

___ ___ ___ ___ ___   ___ ___ ___ ___ ___ ___ ___

✒ ✏ ❀ ✳ ✿   ✂ ✿ ♣ ✂ ✳ ✿ ❦

2. Many Indians chose to stay on their reservations and not move to the city. They thought that if they moved to the city, they would lose the way of life that their parents and ancestors had taught. These Indians called themselves:

___ ___ ___ ___ ___ ___ ___ ___ ___ ___ ___   ___ ___ ___ ___ ___ ___ ___

✏ ➸ ❦ ➸ ✏ ✙ ✳ ☎ ✂ ☆ ✿   ✂ ✿ ♣ ✂ ✳ ✿ ❦

3. Native Americans who moved to cities lived close to each other. They tried to keep their way of life as much as possible. They did not want to forget their religion, native art, or music. They did not want to lose their:

___ ___ ___ ___ ___ ___ ___

⌘ ✒ ✈ ☎ ✒ ✏ ➸

4. Are you afraid of heights? Many people are. The Mohawk Indians are not! Many of them work hundreds of feet above the city to build steel frames for skyscrapers. People who do this work above the city are:

___ ___ ___ ___ ___   ___ ___ ___ ___ ___ ___ ___

❦ ☎ ➸ ➸ ✈   ✗ ☆ ✏ ☛ ➸ ✏ ❦

5. Today urban Indians and reservation Indians come together to celebrate their culture. They share ideas and stories. They dance and beat drums. They make and sell Indian jewelry. During these celebrations, Indians remember how much they have to be proud of! These big parties are called

___ ___ ___ ___ ___ ___ ___

✦ ☆ ✗ ✗ ☆ ✗ ❦